MW00844614

WITHDRAWN

SPOTTING DIFFERENCES

Bee or Wasp?

by Kirsten Chang

BELLWETHER MEDIA · MINNEAPOLIS, MN

Note to Librarians, Teachers, and Parents:

Blastoff! Readers are carefully developed by literacy experts and combine standards-based content with developmentally appropriate text.

Level 1 provides the most support through repetition of high-frequency words, light text, predictable sentence patterns, and strong visual support.

Level 2 offers early readers a bit more challenge through varied simple sentences, increased text load, and less repetition of high-frequency words.

Level 3 advances early-fluent readers toward fluency through increased text and concept load, less reliance on visuals, longer sentences, and more literary language.

Level 4 builds reading stamina by providing more text per page, increased use of punctuation, greater variation in sentence patterns, and increasingly challenging vocabulary.

Level 5 encourages children to move from "learning to read" to "reading to learn" by providing even more text, varied writing styles, and less familiar topics.

Whichever book is right for your reader, Blastoff! Readers are the perfect books to build confidence and encourage a love of reading that will last a lifetime!

This edition first published in 2020 by Bellwether Media, Inc.

No part of this publication may be reproduced in whole or in part without written permission of the publisher. For information regarding permission, write to Bellwether Media, Inc., Attention: Permissions Department, 6012 Blue Circle Drive, Minnetonka, MN 55343.

Library of Congress Cataloging-in-Publication Data

Names: Chang, Kirsten, 1991- author.
Title: Bee or Wasp? / by Kirsten Chang.
Description: Minneapolis, MN : Bellwether Media, Inc., [2020] | Series: Blastoff! Readers: Spotting Differences | Audience: Age 5-8. | Audience: K to Grade 3. | Includes bibliographical references and index.
Identifiers: LCCN 2018054607 (print) | LCCN 2018056487 (ebook) |
  ISBN 9781618915726 (ebook) | ISBN 9781644870310 (hardcover : alk. paper)
Subjects: LCSH: Bees--Juvenile literature. | Wasps--Juvenile literature.
Classification: LCC QL565.2 (ebook) | LCC QL565.2 .C43 2020 (print) | DDC 595.79/9--dc23
LC record available at https://lccn.loc.gov/2018054607

Editor: Al Albertson   Designer: Jeffrey Kollock

Printed in the United States of America, North Mankato, MN.

Table of Contents

Bees and Wasps   4

Different Looks   8

Different Lives   14

Side by Side   20

Glossary   22

To Learn More   23

Index   24

Bees and Wasps

Bees and wasps are both small **insects**. They fly with two pairs of wings.

bees

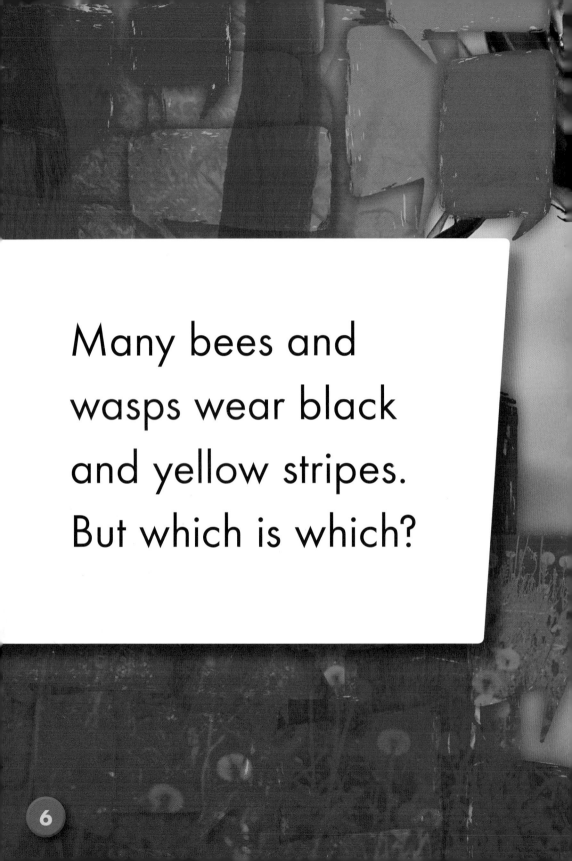

Many bees and wasps wear black and yellow stripes. But which is which?

wasp

Bees are covered in tiny hairs. Wasps look smooth and shiny.

hair

These insects have **similar** colors. But bees are dull. Wasps are bright!

Wasps have bodies that are thin in the middle. Bees have round bodies.

Bees collect **nectar** from plants. They turn it into honey! Wasps do not make honey.

honey

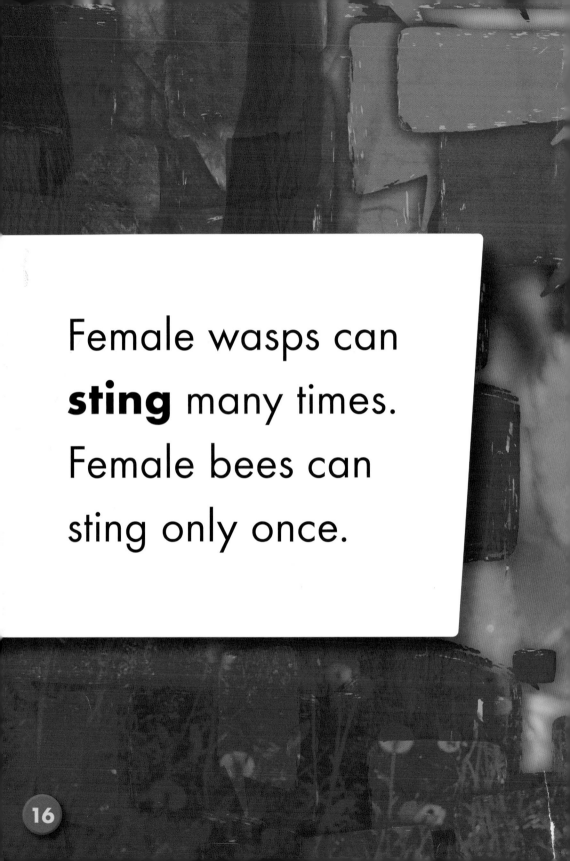

Female wasps can **sting** many times.
Female bees can sting only once.

wasp
stinger

Bees live in **hives** or nests. Wasps live in paper nests. Can you tell the difference?

dull colors

round
body

tiny
hairs

Bee Differences

make
honey

live in hives
or nests

can sting
once

smooth
body

long, thin
body

bright
colors

Wasp Differences

do not
make
honey

live in
paper nests

can sting
many times

Glossary

hives

the homes of bees

similar

close to the same

insects

small animals with six legs and hard outer bodies

sting

to prick painfully

nectar

a sweet liquid that comes from plants, especially flowers

To Learn More

AT THE LIBRARY

Latta, Sara L. *Bees and Wasps: Secrets of Their Busy Colonies*. North Mankato, Minn.: Capstone Press, 2019.

Leaf, Christina. *Honeybees*. Minneapolis, Minn.: Bellwether Media, 2018.

Perish, Patrick. *Wasps*. Minneapolis, Minn.: Bellwether Media, 2018.

ON THE WEB

FACTSURFER

Factsurfer.com gives you a safe, fun way to find more information.

1. Go to www.factsurfer.com.

2. Enter "bee or wasp" into the search box and click 🔍.

3. Select your book cover to see a list of related web sites.

Index

bodies, 12

colors, 10

females, 16

fly, 4

hairs, 8, 9

hives, 18

honey, 14, 15

insects, 4, 10

nectar, 14

nests, 18

plants, 14

sting, 16, 17

stripes, 6

wings, 4

The images in this book are reproduced through the courtesy of: Daniel Prudek, front cover (bee); Luc Pouliot, front cover (wasp); RUKSUTAKARN studio, pp. 4-5; Gregory Johnson, pp. 6-7; Sergey Lavrentev, pp. 8-9; Cornel Constantin, p. 9 (hair); nechaevkon, pp. 10-11; Dmitri Gomon, p. 11 (bubble); IRINA ORLOVA, pp. 12-13; Gelner Tivadar, p. 13 (bubble); StudioSmart, pp. 14-15; Pavel Krasensky, pp. 16-17; Craig Taylor, p. 17 (stinger); Sarah2, pp. 18-19; irin-k, pp. 20 (bee), 21 (wasp); Anneka, p. 20 (honey); PowerUp, p. 20 (hive); Alta Oosthuizen, p. 20 (stinger); Andrea Geiss, p. 21 (no honey); matteo sani, p. 21 (nest); Irina Kozorog, p. 21 (stinger), 22 (sting); Darios, p. 22 (hive); JSseng, p. 22 (insects); Srijira Ruechapaisarnanak, p. 22 (nectar); Aliaksandr Bukatsich, p. 22 (similar).